Making Our Pact

Lower School Programs for Character Development

Edited by

Jennifer Aanderud

& David Streight

ISBN: 978-1-881678-82-3

Contents

The Importance of a School Pact

David Streight • Executive Director, CSEE

I frequently tell the story of one of my first encounters with a "pact school." I was in an office with a group of administrators and counselors at Isidore Newman School in New Orleans, hearing about the Lower School's good character development work. I hear about good character development frequently, but my special interest is in the extent to which students are aware of the good work their teachers are doing. One of our Florida schools was once generous enough to share data with colleagues indicating that, though 91% of their Lower School teachers maintained they talked about the school's character code in class on a daily basis, only 26% of students reported hearing about the character code that often.

The Isidore Newman program sounded absolutely wonderful. I asked my question unassertively: what would students say if I asked them about "the Newman Way"? Perhaps to her dismay, a fourth-grader happened to be walking past the door. "Grab that girl," the Lower School head hurriedly whispered. It was October or November, and the girl just happened to be a new student, thus only in her third month at the school. She got the question despite her short tenure: "Could you tell this gentleman about the Newman Way?"

What ensued was an articulate, age appropriate, explanation that the Newman Way is a community agreement, that school works best if we all treat one another the same way, that everybody should treat others with respect and kindness, that all should be responsible and honest. I forget if it was the girl or someone else who pointed out that older students—fourth and fifth graders, in this case—are expected to model the Newman

Way for younger students, and in so doing they become "teachers" and perpetuators of the school's established norms.

This impossible-to-orchestrate scenario was a clincher, of course. I could have not been more impressed than with a new student, caught completely off guard, articulating a vision (and a reality) for a self-perpetuating set of community expectations.

In their book *Building an Intentional School Culture* (2008), Charles Elbot and David Fulton describe a number of schools that have done work similar to Isidore Newman. Elbot and Fulton use the word "touchstone," which they describe as "a central tool for shaping an intentional school culture." A touchstone contains, they say, "universal principles to guide daily decision making, behavior, and reflection." Elbot and Fulton's touchstone schools craft statements that encapsulate the shared values of an educational community. At Teller Elementary School, for example, the Teller Promise affirms that "we learn and laugh together. We respect each other by using kind words and actions. We take responsibility for our own learning and behavior, even when no one is watching. At Teller, we celebrate each other's differences and accomplishments" (p. 37). Edison Elementary's touchstone is even simpler: "At Edison we are: Community minded, Aware, Responsible, Respectful, Empathetic, Safe. Together we learn. Together we grow. Together we achieve" (p. 36).

Character educators Tom Lickona and Rich Parisi (2009) describe touchstones—also referred to as pacts, ways, contracts, compacts or a variety of other terms— as expressing "the core values of the organization"; a touchstone helps its members "feel connected to each other through these values." Pacts form "the glue that holds the organization together and keeps it focused, even during turbulent times" (p. 37).

> " *Pacts form 'the glue that holds the organization together and keeps it focused, even during turbulent times.'* "

Through CSEE's work with independent schools, we have become aware of a handful of institutions that have managed to craft such cultures: cultures that, at their best, build community, teach socio-moral competence, further moral growth, and give students the kinds of meaningful roles to play that foster both attachment to school today, and loyal, appreciative alums for tomorrow. In most cases, the schools we highlight in this short book have not elaborated touchstones as lengthy as Edison or Teller; they have rather taken a shorter road. For example, all students and faculty at The Peck School (NJ) need to say is "InDeCoRe" (pronounced in-decor), and community members read the shorthand: INdividual DEcisions that affect COmmunity REsponsibility. At Brentwood School (CA), the simple term "Community of Care" already encapsulates the school's core values, which everyone knows. At Breck (MN), everyone in the lower school knows what "C.A.R.E." means.

Though the programs outlined in this booklet are diverse, they share a deep commonality that, we hope, others will work to emulate. This commonality entails a set of community norms that all ascribe to: norms informing a school culture that is perpetuated as much by student-to-student transfer as it is by adult-to-student teaching. A moral school culture is not viable until it has buy-in and participation from both adults and students. The results are worth the effort.

> **A moral school culture is not viable until it has buy-in and participation from both adults and students.**

What the best of the programs in this booklet share is both breadth and depth. By breadth I refer to the fact that most of these schools have identified goals that are spread across a student's experience regardless of what grade he or she is in. A student giving a tour at Kent Denver School in Colorado, for example, once explained why students could not help but know the school's core values: besides regular reminders from the head of school and the presence of core values in classroom discussions, "even the coaches talk about them." The core values at Isidore Newman—respect, responsibility, honesty and kindness—are not just addressed in classroom visits by the school counselor and mentioned in assemblies; they enter into science lessons and language arts discussions; they inform behavior on the playground and in the lunch room; and they get sent home in notes to parents with suggestions for how they can be discussed at home. One teacher might be addressing respect and kindness in relation to a history lesson while another is addressing responsibility and honesty as students begin to learn how to research. They are, in essence, woven into the fabric of the school.

There is a thread of depth that also runs through many of these programs, where we see one skill building on another. We see a version of this in Greensboro Day's teaching younger students to identify simple feelings, while in later grades the program helps students process the experience of having more than one feeling at a time. At Isidore Newman, the goal is for fifth graders to play a leadership role. After five or six years, the Lower School wants its older students to take responsibility for passing along Newman's culture. So even though the core values are distributed broadly across the whole program, there is also a progressive thread that begins with pre-kindergartners and runs through students' departure for Middle School. Students learn to identify feelings, and then to manage feelings; a year or two later they engage with the concept that others might have feelings different from theirs, and that others' feelings must be respected; in second and third grade the focus is on managing friendships, on solving conflict in friendships, and on building community; fourth graders learn about choices, and fifth graders assume responsibility for being models and teachers for those younger. At all levels, respect, responsibility, honesty and kindness are still central; some values might be demonstrated differently at different ages, but they are nevertheless essential at the school.

Though we do not hold the schools here up as perfection, nor do they, we do look at them as deserving notice, precisely because they have taken intentional steps: they have thought through and focused on goals that are supported and endorsed by the community; they have visions shared by all constituents (faculty, students, trustees, parents); they have managed to weave their visions deeply into the fabric of the school; and they are on-going, dynamic programs constantly open to fine-tuning.

None of these schools would be comfortable with our considering them paragons of excellence. Each will admit it has work to do; each avows multiple areas where things could be better. In some cases, the schools featured here have tremendous success at one level (most are lower school programs), but transfer to later divisions has been less than complete. Different schools encounter different obstacles. That being said, both we at CSEE and the authors of the chapters here hope that the ideas presented will be helpful in strengthening programs in lots of schools.

David Streight
Executive Director
Center for Spiritual and Ethical Education

References

Elbot, C. & Fulton, D. (2008) *Building an Intentional School Culture: Excellence in Academics and Character.* Thousand Oaks, California: Corwin Press

Lickona, T. and Parisi, R. (2009). "The Power of a Touchstone," in Streight, D. (ed) *Good Things to Do: Expert Suggestions for Fostering Goodness in Kids.* Portland, CSEE Publications.

The Newman Way

Isidore Newman School • New Orleans, Louisiana
Penny B. Evins, M.Ed. & Sheila Korones Gold, LCSW, RPT

Isidore Newman School is a century-old, K-12 school with just under 450 students in the Lower School. As a new lower school head in 2006, Penny Evins soon realized she had come to a school where fantastic things were happening, but in isolation and "without common needle and thread to create a quilt." To some, the school did not feel like the community they so needed and wanted; the faculty, the students, the school as a whole, were hungry for community building opportunities.

What the Lower School needed could not depend on Evins' vision alone, of course. Her task was to keep the school's outstanding legacy intact, but to help the Lower School faculty pull together all that had been integral to that legacy. She listened at length, in part via extensive interviews with her faculty; she looked for the common messages regarding the work faculty were engaged in; she synthesized their thoughts. Evins described the essence of the work her faculty was to do as road construction for the future drivers. The Lower School was where the road to the future began. They were not teaching AP Chemistry, but they were shaping the filter through which all thoughts, acts, and deeds of the next generation would flow.

What the Lower School needed was a climate-building character education program that was more comprehensive than the hodgepodge pockets of individual greatness that already existed. It did not need a program that depended on a particular teacher's skill or personality, or on a year in a certain class, or on a character trait of the week. What Newman's Lower School needed was a cohesive roadmap from point A to point B. What they ended up with they called the Newman Way.

The Program and How the Process Began

The Newman Way is based on Isidore Newman School's core values: honesty, kindness, respect, and responsibility. The messages Evins heard in her faculty and staff interviews frequently came back to these four values. In a sense, they already were a part of the school; but they needed to be highlighted.

Guidance counselor Sheila Gold arrived at Newman the year before Penny Evins, and the two shared a passion and interest in instilling the school's core values both widely and deeply. Gold committed to work with the Newman Way in every classroom in Lower School during her regular classroom visits. Her goal each day was seen as helping "develop citizens of our community that make a difference." From the beginning, her intention has been to have each student develop a greater sense of empathy: a personal quality often seen as the vitamin that will help students succeed in an increasingly interconnected world.

As teachers filed in for their annual gathering to being the school year, they were divided into grade level teams. Each team was handed a stack of newspapers, a role of duct tape and a brick. With newspaper and tape, they had 30 minutes to construct a bridge capable of supporting the brick. When finished, each grade level

> ❝ *The entire faculty must work in concert to make the transition from one bridge to the next as seamless as possible.* ❞

"mini bridge" had to connect to the bridge built by the team of teachers in the grades above and below them, thus creating one large bridge. In other words, the second grade teachers created a bridge that linked with the first grade bridge, as well as to the structure made by the third grade team. Though all enjoyed the activity, the question "why" remained unanswered. The fruit of the group's labor was symbolic in and of itself; grade level teachers were creating a series of "bridges," each supporting students and at the same time preparing them for the challenges they would find crossing the next bridge. The entire faculty must work in concert to make the transition from one bridge to the next as seamless as possible.

The process revealed much. It served to demonstrate the "Newman Way." It brought many of the school's core values—honesty, kindness, respect and responsibility—to the forefront. In later reflection, teachers spoke about how they approached the project and how individuals treated one another along the journey. Some teams sent "scouts" to see what the other grade levels were doing. Was this honest? Some groups only had a few members involved in the process. Was this kind and respectful? Were all opinions heard? Are we able to model for our students the same behavior that we expect from them? The hands-on exercise became a metaphor for teamwork toward a mutual goal, but the exercise also left room for creativity. Similarly, the "Newman Way" is expressed uniquely from classroom to classroom, but each and every class promotes the singular goal of treating all members of the community with honesty, kindness respect and responsibility: the four points on the Newman moral compass.

What the Newman Way Looks Like and How It Works

Isidore Newman School's shared values are the foundation of the Lower School culture and they strive towards these ideals:

- We live and learn by our four core values.

- We support each other. We believe in each other. We acknowledge and respect each other.

- We push for academic and personal excellence.

- We can all improve and learn from one another; mistakes are the best teachers.

- There are no second-class citizens.

- We are an open society.

- Empathy for the other student is not a weakness.

- We depend upon one another.

- Try not to ask someone to do something you would not do yourself.

- We run to problems, not away from them, when appropriate.

- We hold high standards of moral and ethical behavior.

- We are a warm, close community. This is a strength, not a weakness.

After coming to the school, Gold developed and continues to fine-tune a guidance curriculum to teach feelings, conflict resolution, ways to be considerate of others and the skills of friendship. She wanted students to learn to see themselves as members of a greater whole. The Newman Way was envisioned as an environment of value, where all members of the school community are appreciated for their individuality as well as for the special gifts they add; the whole is greater than the sum of its parts.

> **The Newman Way was envisioned as an environment of value, where all members of the school community are appreciated for their individuality as well as for the special gifts they add.**

Gold's piece of the curriculum is fun, hands-on and experiential. A registered play therapist, she works in all class settings and allows the students to build a set of skills, to find their personal voices and develop positive ways to interact, and to solve interpersonal problems when they arise. Most importantly, she sees the curriculum as being put together sequentially.

In pre-kindergarten and kindergarten, the themes for the year are identifying feelings, and how to talk about feelings. They are read, and then discussed, in books like Elizabeth Burdick's *Words Are Not for Hurting*, Trace Moroney's *When I'm Feeling Sad*, and Peggy Snow's *Feelings to Share from A to Z*. In the first grade the focus is on empathy—on being attentive to the feelings of others—and on building community. Among other things, they create a chain out of strips of paper and, on each link, students write something that could be said to someone to make the person feel good. Newman's core values—honesty, respect, responsibility and kindness—are woven into both talk and activities throughout.

In the second grade, discussions and lessons throughout the year focus on the skills of making and keeping friends. Students look at what kinds of actions boost friendships, and what tends to tear them apart. They learn the power of apologies. The friendship theme continues into third grade when more specific work is done on problem solving and conflict resolution.

Fourth- and fifth-graders at Newman are given progressive responsibility as role models for younger students. The work with kindergartners on feelings and recognizing feelings in others, and in later grades on friendship and community building, is progressively leading to the fifth-grade theme of leadership and personal responsibility. By the time students reach these two upper grades of the Lower School, they have learned how their younger schoolmates are both looking up to them and relying on their modeling so that they, in turn, can learn to live and teach the Newman Way.

Fourth graders thus spend the year with a focus on "choices." The older they get, the more decisions they need to make. They look at role models and the way others influence their decisions. They realize the responsibility of choices, and they look at how Newman's four core values—kindness, responsibility, honesty, and respect—both impact and are impacted by the choices they make. By the time they are in the fifth grade, they should be ready for full responsibility in the Lower School. They should be ready to look at ways they, too, can lead using Newman's core values and thus exemplify the Newman Way for those in grades below them.

Under Evins' leadership, work to ingrain the Newman Way is deeply reinforced by individual classroom teachers. Core values and the Way itself are woven into classroom projects and lessons in a variety of creative ways. It is rare to enter a Lower School classroom without seeing, displayed somewhere, a representation of the Newman Way, what it means, and how it is relevant both to life and to what students are learning at the school.

> *Core values and the Way itself are woven into classroom projects and lessons in a variety of creative ways.*

Ultimately, the Newman Way permeates lives far beyond the classroom. It is part of the lexicon of the Lower School. The Newman Way Principal's Award is given yearly to an outstanding fifth grade student who embodies the school's core values and Newman Way bracelets (green rubber) are given to each student on the first day of school. The Newman Way is discussed in Admission Forums and Newman Way cards are given to students by adults in the community who "catch" a student behaving in a way that exemplifies the Newman Way. This might entail holding the door open for a friend, helping a fellow student up if he or she has fallen, or simply sharing a snack when a classmate has forgotten to bring something from home. The students who receive Newman Way cards have their names called during Lower School assemblies every month. Students are also encouraged to write cards for each other, for guest speakers, or for other community members; and parents write them for other parents.

All actions are viewed through the lens of core values: honesty, kindness respect and responsibility.

> " *All actions are viewed through the lens of core values: honesty, kindness, respect and responsibility.* "

Parents also have roles to play. They receive monthly notes from the guidance counselor reporting what she has been doing with their children in the classroom. The monthly notes often remind parents of the core values and their importance to school culture. More importantly, the monthly notes suggest ways that parents can follow up on work done at school. For example, if Gold has recently read Trudy Ludwig's *Sorry* to second graders and discussed with them the differences between a sincere apology and one that is just words, the note home will encourage parents to ask their children about the art of the apology and to share what they learned in class.

The Newman Way has been so well integrated—to the point where the word pervasive might arise—that Lower School teachers at Newman have (rightfully) wondered if they have been "branding too much," if they have been overdoing the links to core values and the Way. More often than not, observations of students have offered the answer. On the playground, in the lunch line, after leaving the restroom, teachers hear student language: "It's The Newman Way to share." "It is The Newman Way to wait your turn."

Assessing Progress

As the last paragraph above suggests, evaluation of the program has been ongoing and thoughtful, at least informally, during the early years as the Newman Way was developed and implemented. Recently, the Lower School has looked more carefully into the advantages of doing additional assessment regarding their areas of strength and weakness, and a first survey was filled out by students, parents, faculty and staff during the 2011-12 school year. The data was helpful because it offered an opportunity for the three constituencies confidentially to share their feedback about the impact that The Newman Way has had on the community. They learned that there is overwhelming support for character education at

Newman and that all members of the Lower School population perceive a kinder, warmer and more compassionate ethos as a result of a shared value system. Even with varying suggestions for tweaking, the conversation is occurring and this in and of itself puts focus on the why behind the what that is done. The process of evaluating and synthesizing information caused them to think about the character education and therein, provided yet another opportunity for them to craft time for discussions of moral education.

Penny B. Evins, M.Ed., *is Lower School head at Isidore Newman School. She has served as an administrator in all divisions of independent schools. Passionate about character education, community building and leading through service, she feels privileged to have had the fortune of working with, connecting, and learning from others. Penny shares her life, time and love with her husband, son, daughter, and extended family.*

Sheila Korones Gold, LCSW, RPT, *is Lower School guidance counselor at the School. She is a licensed clinical social worker and a registered play therapist, and the author of CSEE's publication* Finding Your Way: A Play-Based Guide to Character Development in Schools. *Sheila shares her life with her husband and two daughters, enjoying friends, New Orleans and offering her time to support her community.*

A Community of Caring

Brentwood School • Los Angeles, California
Laura Taylor Stahoski, MSW, LCSW & Cassandra Clarke, M.Ed.

Brentwood is a K-12 school that has become prominent in the Los Angeles independent school community. In addition to its academic reputation, Brentwood's dedication to character education has provided an exceptionally nurturing learning environment for the 300 students in the K-6 lower division. Brentwood presents students with meaningful experiences that teach them self-awareness, empathy to the experiences of others, and ethical action. The school was honored with the distinction of being a California State School of Character in both 2010 and 2011 and, also in 2011, with being named a National School of Character by the Character Education Partnership.

The Program and How the Process Began

The foundation of Brentwood's Community of Caring program is based on the six core values of community, caring, respect, trust, honesty, and responsibility. These core values have been an integral part of the school since 1999. Initially, a number of character education programs were reviewed for adoption. The Eunice Kennedy Shriver National Center for Community of Caring Program was chosen because it held a high standard for teaching children to be moral, ethical, and caring members of a society, while allowing for a flexible approach to implementation. Upon careful reflection, a variety of Brentwood stakeholders, including the director, school counselor, and selected faculty, modified the original program to better match the needs of the school. For example, the original core value of *family* was changed to *community* with the intent of engendering a more inclusive and interconnected sensibility about who the beneficiaries of the program were. Those involved in the initial review of the program also agreed to add *honesty* to the original list of core values.

When designing the character education program, the administration at Brentwood committed to teaching the core values through class meetings held every Friday from 12:20 p.m. to 1:00 p.m. Each grade breaks into groups of eight to ten students and, whether the groups take to the field, to hallways, or remain in the classrooms, the entire Lower Division is

> **"** *Students see that the entire faculty is invested in the character education program and is present to support students...* **"**

quietly engaged in value-based discussions. The smaller group format has been particularly helpful for students who may be hesitant to share their feelings within a whole class discussion. Individual groups are facilitated by teachers and administrators. Students see that the entire faculty is invested in the character education program and is present to support students both in and out of the group setting.

Since the program was first implemented, the school counselor, who coordinates the character education program, and the director discuss new ideas, themes, activities, lesson plans, and assemblies during the summer in preparation for the new school year. During in-service week prior to the start of school, they take these ideas to the faculty who are encouraged to contribute their thoughts, opinions, and suggestions. The counselor then provides the faculty with a calendar of scheduled topics for weekly class meetings. The original Community of Caring Program has been enhanced over the years, resulting in a self-published "Community of Caring" binder. This binder is used in weekly class meetings where age specific role-playing activities and discussion prompts help the students understand how the core values can be a guide to making "right" rather than "wrong" choices. Faculty and staff members also adhere to the same core values as the students. Specialized training in the Community of Caring Program targeted at incoming faculty and staff during the summer in-service week allows for the school counselor and experienced faculty members to teach the values and methodologies that are integral to the school culture. Character education continues to be planned and discussed throughout the year during faculty meetings, between individual faculty members and administration, as well as via email to the entire faculty.

What a Community of Caring Looks Like and How It Works

Weekly class meetings have been instrumental in fostering positive relationships and helping students learn the value of respecting, trusting, and supporting one another. Class meetings illustrate similarities among students while teaching them to respect and celebrate differences. Students learn the importance of expressing their feelings, listening to others, and problem solving a variety of concerns that arise within the school environment. The depth of class discussions evolves over the course of the year, with student participation becoming increasingly candid and personal in nature. Class meetings use student-generated confidentiality rules and behavioral expectations to develop moral motivation. Students respect the input from their classmates and support one another by offering comfort, validation, and advice. When they disagree with a comment or perception of a situation, they have learned to do so in a respectful manner.

Class meetings also serve to strengthen the student – teacher relationship. As the facilitator, the teacher is better able to understand the social dynamics of his/her students and support individuals with follow up discussions when needed.

As they develop, children's behavior inevitably includes inconsistency and the shifting of friendship circles. Faculty realize that these moments are critical opportunities for children to learn

While the consistent focus on core values and the weekly Community of Caring meetings help to provide students with an emotionally safe campus and increasing levels of self-efficacy and autonomy, it would be unrealistic to imagine a totally conflict-free zone. As children develop, their behavior inevitably includes inconsistency and the shifting of friendship circles. Faculty realize that these moments are critical opportunities for children to learn about themselves by finding a voice to express their feelings, as well as to develop their listening skills. All students are taught the Brentwood Lower Division's conflict resolution process, which can easily be followed to solve arguments with the proceeding six steps:

- Cool Off/Calm Down

- Use "I" Messages

- Express Your Needs

- Brainstorm Solutions

- Make a Plan, and

- Do It

At times, students need a little more assistance in resolving differences positively, and adults are always available to assist. Aside from the classroom teachers who are trained in the conflict resolution strategies, the school counselor is available to help students navigate the occasionally turbulent waters of grade school and discuss alternatives when there is conflict. Faculty are visible on the playground during recess and often eat lunch with students, further reinforcing relationships while enabling them to gain added insight into the social lives of students. Teacher presence on the playground allows for consistent emphasis on teaching, encouraging, and modeling of effective problem solving and conflict resolution skills. Teachers praise behaviors that espouse the core values and connect with and re-direct students who are experiencing difficulties.

Recognizing that children develop at varying rates in both their cognitive and emotional functioning motivates the Lower Division's dedication to providing differentiated learning opportunities. However, this does not mean that unsocial or unkind behavior is tolerated. Children are encouraged to see that their choices and actions lead to consequences so they begin to internalize the lesson that positive actions reap beneficial rewards and negative choices have the opposite result. The key to this approach is to encourage self-reflection in the process of making choices and assessing consequences. When a child fills out a Brentwood Cares form and discusses it with a parent or teacher, s/he is always asked to identify how s/he contributed to the situation, to reflect upon any decisions, and envision better choices for the future. Conversely, if a student experiences a positive event, s/he is encouraged to reflect upon how ethical behavior and constructive choices resulted in that outcome. Students are praised for choices that show ethical behavior; rather than receiving generic or material recognition, the hope is that they will learn to appreciate the positive feelings that develop intrinsically.

Another vital facet of the character program is monthly assemblies. Throughout the year, each grade is responsible for leading one assembly. Aside from serving to introduce the specific core value that will be the focus of upcoming Friday class meetings, assemblies foster students' creativity and a sense of community. For example, third grade invited other grades, as well as their Head Start buddies, to share the stage as they sang about the importance of trust, respect, and community. Assemblies are also occasionally used to introduce new and exciting additions to the character program. Recently, the sixth grade leadership team collaborated with students and teachers on the Community of Caring Action Committee designed to enhance the Community of Caring program. They created Contain-It Cubes where students could deposit questions or concerns written anonymously, because they realized that some students are hesitant to voice feelings during class meetings. At the assembly, the students presented each class with a Contain-It Cube and shared a video that included examples of questions or concerns to place in the box, as well as questions and concerns that would be answered more appropriately through another avenue. This informative and entertaining assembly exemplifies the organic and dynamic nature of Brentwood's character program.

The Lower Division's service learning program at Brentwood is intricately tied into the Community of Caring program. As the service learning coordinator said, "The service learning program is all about putting the core values into action." Service projects are linked to grade level curriculum and the core values, and include a student run campus recycling program, distributing lunches to the homeless, sponsoring fundraisers for international relief organizations, accompanying disabled children to a wheelchair accessible playground, visiting centers for the aged, and cleaning a regional summer camp for chronically ill children. The coordinator holds initial class meetings where Brentwood's purpose and expectations of service are clearly communicated. Reflection meetings, where students discuss and journal their experiences, are held after each service project. Brentwood also holds seven school drives

> " *The service learning program is all about putting the core values into action.* "

throughout the year to benefit various outside organizations, in addition to organizing service trips for faculty.

Brentwood's character education goals are incorporated into all academic disciplines. Each grade level selects and continuously assesses its core literature program to ensure that materials provide opportunities for rich ethical discussions to aid in the development of moral reasoning. For example, fifth graders read *Petey* by Ben Mikaelsen, which integrates with the service learning curriculum. All grade levels emphasize the values by incorporating multi-cultural curriculum, such as the third grade's theme of Travels the Globe, which exposes students to a variety of world cultures, geography, and history. Teachers highlight the core values through direct questioning, writing prompts that elicit student expression of the values, and other teachable moments. In science, teachers emphasize how respect is a key to environmental investigations, while art teachers provide activities that demonstrate how a community of students can create collaborative pieces.

> **"** *Each grade level selects and continuously assesses its core literature program to ensure that materials provide opportunities for rich ethical discussions to aid in the development of moral reasoning.* **"**

Students have many opportunities to live the core values outside the classroom as well, through student government, sports, and other programs. The extra-curricular sports programs incorporate core values with goal-setting and post-game reflections. Student athletes and coaches sign a code of ethics agreement that emphasizes core values such as respect (of teammates, other players, officials, and coaches) responsibility (safety as a repeated top priority), honesty (adhering to rules), caring (emphasizing constructive criticism and discretion) and community (valuing and respecting the relationship with teammates, supporters, and school facilities).

There are numerous ways in which the school fosters caring attachments among students. Brentwood offers a week of Kindercamp the summer before students start kindergarten. This week of team building activities familiarizes students with the campus and with one another, easing transitions when school begins. In addition, older grades are buddied with younger grades where a variety of activities provide cross-age experiences; and recesses are purposefully scheduled to do the same.

Regular assemblies and musical presentations consistently provide opportunities for students of all ages to appreciate and applaud each other. Affinity groups, such as the Crayon Box, are open to all students, offering camaraderie and support as themes of diversity and identity are explored. Students are encouraged to engage collaboratively within the classroom throughout the day, whether in games or academic lessons. Brentwood annually participates in the National Mix It Up Day, consisting of a day of activities where cross-age groupings of students learn about others as they step out of their comfort zones. Every year, the fifth grade students go on an overnight field trip where the sole emphasis is on team building, community bonding, and collaborative problem solving.

Brentwood also fosters caring attachments among the adults within the school community. Brentwood parents participate in social gatherings such as family potlucks and parent affinity groups. Teachers' personal milestones such as birthdays, engagements, weddings, and births are celebrated with Social Committee sponsored celebrations. When a loss or setback is suffered in the greater community, the Social Committee is appropriately and sympathetically responsive. Additionally, if any Brentwood School community member is hospitalized or suffers from a death in the family, hot meals are sent to that household for a prolonged time period as a supportive measure. Many faculty and staff members' lives have been enhanced by the school-subsidized, on-site licensed daycare facility for children aged three months to two-and-a-half years.

Assessing Progress

An outside consultant was recently hired to conduct a yearlong study with the goal of ensuring that Brentwood lives up to its Statement of Purpose and provides a nurturing learning environment. When surveyed, 94% of students reported that the faculty and administration know and care about them. In a parent survey, 97% of respondents believed Brentwood School offers a nurturing learning environment and 100% agreed that Brentwood School promotes personal growth. When asked, "What I hope never changes," top responses included: community feel-

> **"** *When asked, 'What I hope never changes,' top responses included: community feeling, faculty/student relationships, emphasis on core values, and caring teachers.* **"**

ing, faculty/student relationships, emphasis on core values, and caring teachers.

The school's Wellness Committee spent a year assessing the school's efficacy in promoting positive peer relations and also hired an outside resource to speak about the importance of empathy. In the Lower School, it was determined that class meetings have significantly improved students' abilities to communicate thoughts and feelings, and to share problem solving strategies.

These surveys have led to positive changes within the school environment. For example, one survey revealed that some students chose not to play specific sports during recess because they did not feel they had strong skills and therefore might be selected last for a team. As a result, faculty members frequently engage in play with students during recess. This helps students feel more secure while faculty members model good sportsmanship and show students that they care about their interests.

> *These surveys have led to positive changes within the school environment.*

Students' character development is recorded on individual report cards in addition to being discussed in parent/teacher conferences. School-wide newsletters, parent education coffees, and frequent personal communication between parents and teachers facilitate community collaboration and core value integration. Teachers are annually required to measure their own efforts in implementing character education as part of their individual reviews. Goal setting and performance review meetings with administration include attention to each faculty member's professional and moral development.

In addition to the above, the Lower School engaged in a rigorous evaluation process to ensure that Brentwood adheres to the practices presented in the submitted portfolio before being named a 2011 National School of Character (NSOC).

And finally, a Character Education Action Committee comprised of faculty, administration, parents, and students meets monthly to review topics related to the character education program. Comments and suggestions from these meetings are then taken to full faculty meetings for additional suggestions and implementation strategies. In this manner, Brentwood's character education program is constantly growing and changing. By practicing self-reflection, positive communication, and adhering to the core values, Brentwood students are preparing themselves for a successful future and helping their school create a legacy of leadership in the character education field.

**Laura Taylor Stahoski, MSW, LCSW,** is a Licensed Clinical Social Worker and the counselor and character education coordinator at Brentwood School's Lower Division. For 13 years she has helped to incorporate the core values of caring, respect, trust, responsibility, and honesty into the life of the school community. Laura assists students with conflict resolution, conducts value-based class meetings, facilitates social-skills groups, and is a resource to faculty and parents on students' general mental health and development.

**Cassandra Clarke, M.Ed.,** has 25 years of experience teaching in schools in New York, San Francisco, Los Angeles and Brazil. She spent her childhood primarily attending international schools overseas and strongly believes that schools are important generators for facilitating peaceful coexistence amongst diverse communities on both a local and global scale. She lives in Los Angeles with her husband, son, and unflaggingly rambunctious labrador.

The Cougar Pact

Collegiate School • Richmond, Virginia
Marella Gregory, M.Ed.

Collegiate School was founded in 1915 as an all-girls, Judeo-Christian independent school. In the mid-1950's Collegiate broadened its roots and extended its branches to include boys, a change that was met with many supporters and almost as many detractors. Despite some growing pains throughout the process, Collegiate is thriving. Currently, Collegiate has over 1500 students in kindergarten through grade twelve. The school's five core values lie at the heart of each division: honor, love of learning, excellence, respect, and community.

Though the school mission statement and values are firmly in place, change and growth—often in response to the recommendations of graduates—remain a constant driving force in Collegiate's development. A formidable and ongoing task has been how best to balance long-standing traditions with both current and future needs of students and a changing world.

Collegiate School's graduates from the decade 1990-2000 were surveyed toward the end of the century, and they defined a need for further growth and inclusion at the school. These graduates were living amidst a cultural shift, and called for Collegiate to better prepare its students for the many changes and developments of this newer, more diverse America. There was important work to be done.

Collegiate School thus committed to become a more diverse and inclusive school community. By the mid- to late 1990s, Collegiate made concerted attempts to admit more minority students on the kindergarten entry level and to hire faculty members open to that growth and diversity. The faculty members hired would need to be steeped in the traditions and core values of a school that had been known and revered for its privileged and homogeneous make-up. This newer wave would need to join forces with a seasoned faculty and a long list of alumni to respond to the graduates' call for a Collegiate School that could be both inclusive and reflective of an America growing in multiculturalism, while able to honor its exclusive beginnings and hold fast and firm to its beloved core.

The Program and How the Process Began

Collegiate School's current character education program began in 2002, when a dozen educators started their journey at the well-established school in Richmond, Virginia. When an educator begins at a school that is new to him or her, but already formed and functioning, a prevailing challenge is to bring all he or she has to offer and see how that fits with what is already in place. An important first step is to learn "the lay of the land" by finding the school's mission statement and learning

> **"** *An important first step is to learn the 'lay of the land' by finding the school's mission statement and learning about what lies at the school's core.* **"**

about what lies at the school's core. This new group of educators joined forces with the veteran faculty members to explore the school's core values and how best to reference those values as Collegiate continued its growth and forward thinking.

One response to this formidable task was to focus the Lower School (K-4) guidance program on the five core values while being mindful of the new direction in which the world was moving. Lower School students met regularly with the school counselor to build strong and solid character around these central values. The Lower School guidance program allowed for an integrated approach to the already academically rich environment. Teachers worked collaboratively with the Lower School counselor to weave both tradition and change into the fabric of the school. Today, this K-4th grade program begins with monthly guidance lessons where books are read with the school's youngest students in order to introduce the values in a fun and relaxing manner. The hope is that students might enjoy and cherish their time spent both learning about and integrating these values into their daily lives and their changing world.

The program culminates with third and fourth grade students writing their own value based character education books, which they can reference and take with them as they graduate from the Lower School.

> " *The program culminates with third and fourth grade students writing their own value based character education books...* "

A celebratory intercultural potluck dinner with faculty members and fourth grade families serves to mark the completion of the students' lower school values studies and to launch them toward their middle school years for continued growth and development.

What the Cougar Pact Looks Like and How It Works

The program has evolved from an exploration and practice of Collegiate School's traditional values to student made books called *Character Education*. The title of the book, however, like the program itself, has evolved. Welcomed change over the most recent part of the decade invites students to be part of Collegiate's "Cougar Pack" as they commit to what is now known as the "Cougar Pact," a promise to incorporate honor, love of learning, excellence, respect, and community into their daily routine.

Some books used to introduce and discuss these five values on the kindergarten-second grade levels are:

- *Jumanji* by Chris Van Allsburg
  (Respect and love of learning: listening skills and following directions)

- *Zathura* by Chris Van Allsburg
  (Respect for others: who is the bully and the victim?)

- *Stand Tall Molly Lou Melon* by Patty Lovell
  (Respect for self)

- *Liar, Liar, Pants on Fire* by Diane deGroate
  (Honor and love of learning: making mistakes as a learner and knowing that the truth always comes out)

- *How to Lose All Your Friends* by Nancy Carlson
  (Community and respect: some do's and don'ts of making and
  keeping friends)

- *Enemy Pie* by Derek Munson
  (Community and respect)

- *The Secret of the Peaceful Warrior* by Dan Millman
  (Honor, respect, and community)

- *A-Z Do You Ever Feel Like Me?* by Bonnie Hausman & Sandi Fellman
  (Respect for self and others)

Finally...

- *Cougar Pact* by each third and fourth grade Collegiate School student (excellence, honor, love of learning, respect, and community)

As teachers return to pick up their students from each monthly guidance lesson, a brief oral review of the lesson in Question & Answer format is conducted. This allows students to share with their teacher what they have learned as well as

> **Teachers help to make each value study relevant to specific class experiences.**

ways they can implement the values into their school day. Teachers help to make each value study relevant to specific class experiences. Input from classroom teachers serves to keep the lessons meaningful.

Another key component of the Lower School program is what the children like to call "Spies and Tattletales." The guidance office offers coveted seating for six to eight children in the form of a large overstuffed sectional couch. As each guidance lesson begins, the students who were seated on the couch in the previous month's lesson are seated there again and asked to report on their month of "spying" on their classmates. Each student selects a peer to take his or her place on the couch by "telling" or reporting specific behaviors they have spotted since the last guidance lesson that illustrate the values studied.

For example:

"I pick David to take my place on the couch because he listened with respect to the teacher and to his classmates. He kept his body still and looked at the person who was speaking."

"Sarina can take my place on the couch because sometimes at recess when I don't have anyone to play with she'll invite me to play, which helps me to feel included and part of our class community."

"Ella showed excellence when she wouldn't give up even though reading was hard for her. She kept trying and trying. She always turns in a completed reading log."

Once new students are seated on the couch, the new value study begins. A story is read and discussed, then students are asked to give examples of what this particular value might look like throughout their daily activities. A review is conducted upon the teacher's return, and students set off to practice the new value with the hopes of being "caught" or "spied upon" by a classmate for next month's lesson. Students, therefore, work daily and monthly to practice each value while looking routinely for examples of that same value in their classmates' behavior. They are encouraged to "look with their eyes and their brains rather than their mouths" in order to instill a thoughtful awareness of attempts being made to practice the values.

> *Students, therefore, work daily and monthly to practice each value while looking routinely for examples of that same value in their classmates' behavior.*

The program takes a different direction after second grade when third and fourth grade students become engaged in creating their own hardcover books as opposed to listening to and discussing many of the sample books mentioned previously. The stories read aloud to kindergarten-second grade, however, often become favorites and are frequently in demand. As third and fourth grade students participate in monthly guidance lessons and work to develop their own values guide, they frequently ask whether or not some of the books they enjoyed in their earlier school years might be read again upon completion of their work.

Some examples of third and fourth grade activities for each value studied that are included in the student-made books are as follows:

Honor:

1) Have students share aloud specific situations they might have experienced in which "doing the right thing" was not necessarily an easy thing to do. After some small group discussions, ask each student to use two pages in his/her *Cougar Pact* book to write and illustrate his/her own story in which he/she learned the value of honor and integrity. Students

can use any form of the following words as part of the story: truth, lie, feel, learn.

2) Using the examples shared by students, invite students to choose five situations to illustrate both honorable and dishonorable choices made. The children write a sample for each in one of five empty balloons, and, using a color coded key, they show that they know the difference between what is honorable or dishonorable.

Love of Learning:

1) Discuss with the class how curiosity leads to continued growth and learning. Have students list three or more specific things about which they are curious.

2) Conduct a class discussion about making mistakes, and how this is often a necessary and valuable part of learning. Review the strategy of how when we make a mistake it often helps to admit it, fix it, and move forward with some new awareness that will be helpful in meeting similar situations in the future. Students include a page in their books, with paw print image, listing the steps to this strategy for future reference.

Excellence:

1) This particular value can be tied into the idea of being willing to make and learn from our mistakes. Have the students write the word "Excellence" (large) across the span of two pages. Then, have students include two interpretations of excellence: striving to be *the* best versus *my* best. Discuss why and how the two concepts are different, and how excellence does not mean perfection.

2) Use the example of each entry in a student's book as being an exercise in excellence. Discuss the unique designs and expressions students have displayed throughout the activities shared and recorded in each *Cougar Pact* book.

Respect:

1) Have students participate in an ABC activity in which they share talents, abilities, interests, etc., that help to show what qualities one might respect in one's self. For example: A is for athlete, B is for brave, C is for caring. One caveat here... no negatives allowed! Have each student do a two page A-Z listing of things he or she might value or respect.

2) Lead a whole class discussion pertaining to the importance and value of respecting differences as just being different, opposed to differences as "weird," "dumb," or "silly." Tie that in with the concept that each person—no matter how different—has worth. Note this in the book.

Community:

1) Read the book *Me on the Map* by Joan Sweeney to introduce the concept that we can consider our location from many different perspectives at the same moment (our bedroom, home, neighborhood, city, etc.). Explore how it is possible for us to be a member in a variety of communities as well, beginning with the family unit and approaching a more global perspective. Have students illustrate the many communities of which they are a part (including some ancestry and heritage). Discuss the concept of interconnectedness. These two pages are titled "Our World Connects Us."

2) Review and illustrate a minimum of 10 community service projects students may have participated in during time spent in the Lower School. Have the students use two pages to trace their hands allowing space (fingers) to list community service projects. Note that there may be times when we need support from others. Title this page "Lend a Helping Hand."

On the first or second Tuesday of the month of May, fourth graders and their families are invited to Collegiate Lower School's annual International Potluck Dinner to honor and celebrate the completion of their values study and Cougar Pact book in the Lower School. Cinco de Values translates to "five values" or "the fifth of the values," which happens to be community. The evening serves to put an emphasis not only on the fourth grade community, but on the many communities around the world from which we all have come.

> *The evening is an opportunity for students to celebrate community, exercise the values they have studied for the past five years, and experience a 'taste' of the many communities from which we are a part.*

Each family is asked to bring a dish from a country of their origin. Dishes are placed on several long serving tables and arranged in order of appetizers, salads, entrees, and desserts. Name cards are used to label and identify the dish, ingredients, and country of origin. The evening is an opportunity for students to celebrate community, exercise the values they have studied for the past five years, and experience a "taste" of the many communities of which they are a part.

Assessing Progress

Evaluation of and adjustments to the program occur annually by adjusting entries in the *Cougar Pact* books as well as adding or removing books from the K through 2nd grade reading list. Teachers and students are asked monthly how each lesson might be improved upon or changed. Teachers feel comfortable sharing specific incidents as they occur that might offer some teachable moments. These are shared verbally, by e-mail, or by making an appointment with the Lower School counselor.

Another kind of evaluation in discussion form occurs at least twice monthly during a scheduled noon lunch on Wednesdays. A variety of teachers are invited to participate or feel free to invite themselves as needed. There is a "core-four" at most of these lunch meetings. The four are: the school counselor, the counselor assistant, the Lower School chair of academic services, and the Lower School art teacher, who also happens to be the K-12 art director. Other topics are discussed in a collaborative fashion during these "over the hump" lunch meetings as well.

Finally, the head and assistant head of the Lower School meet weekly with the school counselor. The direction of the character education program is discussed as needed. Most recently there has been conversation regarding the possibility of including pieces of the Cougar Pack concept and introducing the newer Cougar Pact name during one of the kindergarten through fourth grade Town Meetings. This will likely occur in the form of a skit created and performed by fourth grade students. Constant re-evaluation on a variety of levels helps to keep this Lower School character education program meaningful and pertinent to the ever changing, forward thinking, continually growing Collegiate School.

> **"** *Constant re-evaluation on a variety of levels helps to keep this Lower School character education program meaningful and pertinent...* **"**

Marella Gregory, M.Ed., is the Lower School counselor at Collegiate School in Richmond, VA. where she is honored to work with parents and other educators to meet the growing and changing needs of children in her community. She speaks frequently with parents and teachers on topics such as "Navigating the Social Scene in the Face of Technology," and the "The Importance of Play." She serves on the school's Community Service Committee and is currently participating in the Spiritual Guidance and Mentorship Training program at Atlantic University. She enjoys spending time with her husband, two daughters, and their dog, Lily.

InDeCoRe

The Peck School • Morristown, New Jersey

Antonia Pelaez

The Peck School is located in the small suburban city of Morristown, approximately 30 driving miles from New York City. Founded in 1893, it is a kindergarten through eighth grade co-educational school with a traditional, structured approach to learning. In the tradition of a family school, parents and faculty work together in partnership to help children develop academically and personally. Peck's rigorous curriculum focuses on developing critical thinking skills and applying the knowledge learned in the classroom to the world beyond its walls.

The Program and How the Process Began

The Peck School recognizes that to be truly successful, good character is essential. The effective utilization of knowledge requires a firm moral compass and solid character values. Developing moral integrity and a clear sense of ethics is as fundamental to a Peck education as building strong academic skills. The integration of an academic education and character development are woven into Peck's Mission Statement:

We believe that in life, knowledge must be guided by values. Through a commitment to character formation and a rigorous and inspirational academic program, The Peck School strives to build in each student the capacity for disciplined learning and consideration of others. With dedicated faculty and families, we prepare our students to succeed in secondary school and to lead healthy, productive, and principled lives.

In response to a social incident in 2002, Peck piloted a character education program entitled "Individual Development and Community Responsibility" (InDeCoRe). The pilot program targeted the grade marked by the incident, as well as the grade above it. It utilized in-class programming for the students as well as special events for the students and parents. The purpose was to solidify the school's partnership with parents to instill values, build morality, and develop character in the children while also teaching them to be responsible and responsive to their community.

Within two years, the positive response to this pilot program resulted in a permanent character education program encompassing all grades. Over time, InDeCoRe has also become the central coordinating entity for all formal and informal character development as well as a backbone for discussions and initiatives in other facets of the school. In essence, InDeCoRe is the school's platform for advocating its core values and is a driving force in promoting the intangibles of character education in all school activities.

" *...InDeCoRe is the school's platform for advocating its core values and is a driving force in promoting the intangibles of character education in all school activities.* "

The development and success of the InDeCoRe program is the result of many factors including teacher support and interest. Critical, however, has been the encouragement and support of the school's administration, particularly the headmaster. As InDeCoRe grew and expanded over time, the school's board of trustees also became an important advocate. At the behest of Peck's headmaster and board of trustees, the InDeCoRe program has twice created and implemented a formal long-range plan. The purpose of these plans was to further enhance the opportunities for all Peck constituents to engage in the development and promotion of good character and a strong community. The plan identified character education goals, defined the venues within the school to achieve these goals, specified action steps, and provided time frames.

What InDeCoRe Looks Like and How It Works

The school's psychologist coordinates the InDeCoRe program on a day-to-day basis. However, the administration of InDeCoRe is a constant collaborative effort involving administrators, faculty, students, and parents. The formal governance of InDeCoRe has evolved over the years and currently consists of an administrative team, faculty team, and student team, with a one to two person overlap across these teams. The administrative committee guides the overall InDeCoRe program, meets once a month and consists of the headmaster, Lower School head, Upper School head, director of faculty development, school psychologist, Lower School lead teacher and Upper School lead teacher. Members of this committee communicate with the board of trustees and represent InDeCoRe in their meetings with other administrators, faculty, parents, and others.

The purpose of the Faculty Team for InDeCoRe Values (FTIV) is to oversee the implementation of the student character education activities. It consists of the Lower School lead teacher, Upper School lead teacher, two additional Lower School teachers, two additional Upper School teachers and the school psychologist. During the summer, this group meets to formulate themes and specific programs for the upcoming year. During the school year, FTIV meets monthly to ensure the implementation of the programming they created during the summer. With the additional benefit of having an InDeCoRe budget, this team acts as a support system for the faculty, offering books, current websites, curriculum opportunities, and activities that foster and promote the core values.

The Peck InDeCoRe Club (PIC) consists of Upper School students, two from each grade, who apply and are selected by the Upper School faculty member who facilitates the club and also sits on FTIV. PIC meets approximately 18 times a year during a period set aside for activities. In addition to offering guidance to the faculty about InDeCoRe programming, the students promote character development among their peers. As examples, PIC has created bulletin boards, produced skits/movies for assemblies, created activities and generated discussion ideas for advisory, as well as designed InDeCoRe t-shirts worn by the entire Peck community.

> *In addition to offering guidance to the faculty about InDeCoRe programming, the students promote character development among their peers.*

There is no formal parent InDeCoRe committee although FTIV members and the administrators of Peck's Parents' Association have worked collaboratively to produce articles for Peck publications and special programming for students and parents. The Parents' Association, along with the two class parents at every grade level, are considered to be InDeCoRe's ambassadors to the rest of the parent body. One faculty member on FTIV is designated as the public relations liaison. That person writes or assigns articles about InDeCoRe for all Peck publications. Developing additional and more formal roles for parent collaboration is a future direction for the InDeCoRe program.

> " *In the Lower School grades, character values are defined, recognized, and reinforced within the students' tangible community.* "

Early in InDeCoRe's evolution, a group of teachers and administrators decided on Peck's six core values after discussing and mapping a plethora of 'grande' and 'piccolo' values. Peck's six core values—respect, responsibility, empathy, honesty, perseverance, and loyalty—are featured one per trimester to allow in-depth consideration. Through direct classroom instruction, these values are examined over a rotating two-year time period and within a specific age appropriate context that allows students to develop a deeper and integrated understanding. In the Lower School grades, character values are defined, recognized, and reinforced within the students' tangible community. Specifically, the kindergarten students consider these values through the context of "self," first and second grade students through the context of "family," and third and fourth grade students through the context of "school." When students reach the Upper School, advisory meets three times per six-day cycle, which allows them to discuss and more deeply integrate the abstract notions of character and community. Specifically, fifth and sixth grade students explore the values through the context of the "local community," while the oldest students, the seventh and eighth graders, use the context of the "global community" to consider the different manifestations of these values.

As framed by best practice models of character education in schools, character and values can be studied in the classroom through discussion and analysis. The development of character, however, is a dynamic and ongoing process that occurs through relationships and across venues. At Peck, character is a part of all school activities and is central in the relationships between and among students, faculty, and parents. As examples, the athletic program encourages all students to develop skills, conditioning, and an appreciation of good health while also developing important values of sportsmanship, collaboration, and self-discipline. Similarly, eighth grade students learn about responsibility as they work in the kindergarten each morning before school begins. All students learn to respect each other's opinions during class discussions. Whether they are working with special needs children during the Upper School activities period, reading about history or helping a classmate, children learn about empathy. The development of character lies at the core of Peck's honor code and disciplinary actions. It is the purpose of the Table Talk Tuesday lunch discussions in which students contemplate a provocative ethical dilemma, question, or story. Throughout the school day, InDeCoRe values are examined and reinforced in academic subjects, free play, and sporting events.

> *[The development of character] is the purpose of the Table Talk Tuesday lunch discussions in which students contemplate a provocative ethical dilemma, question, or story.*

The common platform of Peck's six core values provides the framework for student programming related to bullying, service learning, advisory, and thematic instruction. It is recognized in the annual InDeCoRe Award given to a fourth and eighth grade student who, as nominated by peers, best exemplifies Peck's six core values. Character development serves as the theme for regularly scheduled parent discussion groups and book clubs. It is the topic of "InDeCoRe Corner" articles that appear in each of Peck's publications that are distributed to parents, trustees, donors, and faculty. Finally, the importance of character is highlighted through the summer readings assigned to each student. Family time to nurture connection and character is encouraged each trimester during Kairos Family Night when families are encouraged to unplug and spend quality time together.

Through different formats, Peck's faculty and staff engaged in staff training related to character development and values. Some have participated in CSEE sponsored events including webinars and conferences. All have participated in in-service training programs related to children's development, communicating with parents, and training students in specific skill sets.

Consulting professionals have also conducted trainings and discussions with faculty and administrators on such topics as the ethical issues students face with electronic communications, bullying, and making good choices. Summer readings related to character are offered to all staff and the themes of these books are woven into the milieu and faculty meetings of the following school year.

While InDeCoRe values are fostered daily throughout the school, they are the focus of an intensive week of school programming every winter. Each year, Peck uses the Martin Luther King Jr. holiday as a springboard to a theme based values week. During that week, the school comes together for special assemblies and presentations which have focused on bullying awareness, assertiveness and direct communication as well as on standing up for others and connecting in kindness. The school values are celebrated and reinforced with songs, skits, student made movies as well as discussions in both homerooms and advisory groups. Bracelets are made and distributed to all members of the Peck community to serve as a tangible reminder to live a value-guided life. Daily homelinks are sent to parents to reinforce skill sets introduced in school and assist them in family based discussions. Participating in this InDeCoRe based week, students have a greater sense of empowerment and increased empathy in their interactions with peers and the greater community.

Assessing Progress

Though the impact of a character education program like InDeCoRe is easier to sense than to measure, Peck believes there should be tangible evidence of character development in its students. At the beginning of every report card, there is a section describing specific character related attitudes and behaviors that are age appropriate. This enables parents to receive feedback about their child's character development, which is also a central theme in parent-teacher conferences. The Lower School has a Consideration of Others board, which displays pictures of students who have been recognized by their teachers, and at times, their peers for modeling Peck's values. These students also receive an InDeCoRe bookmark and recognition in a Peck publication. The beginning of the school mission statement, *We believe that in life, knowledge must be guided by values,* is predominantly displayed in the Upper School.

Periodic evaluations regarding the "health" of the school community from the student's perspective is an InDeCoRe initiative, which also provides secondary feedback about the impact of the InDeCoRe program. Approximately every three years, students in the fourth through eighth grade complete what used to be called a 'bullying survey' and has been modified to become a more general climate survey. The qualitative and quantitative information garnered from these surveys provides faculty and staff with insight into those aspects of the students' social environment that will always remain hidden from the adults in the community. Programming and adjustments in InDeCoRe initiatives are made as needed to address the social issues identified from these surveys.

In addition to the various InDeCoRe related meetings (Administrative Committee, FTIV, PIC) where themes, initia-

> *Most notably, 'InDeCoRe' has become a verb, adjective, and noun in the day-to-day Peck vernacular.*

tives, and programming are evaluated, Peck has an informal community feedback system that is critical for the same purpose. Moreover, a wealth of anecdotal evidence speaks to the impact that the InDeCoRe program has had on the Peck community. Most notably, 'InDeCoRe' has become a verb, adjective, and noun in the day-to-day Peck vernacular. For example, the importance of character and values as learned through InDeCoRe was noted in a recent commencement speech given by an eighth grade student. Nonetheless, future consideration is needed regarding evaluation of the InDeCoRe program to ensure its efficacy.

The Peck community is proud of the evolution of the InDeCoRe program, but key to its continued success is having a growth mindset. The faculty and administration will continue to monitor the ever changing community and, with on-going education, collaboration, and dedication, InDeCoRe will grow and change to meet the needs of the students.

Antonia Pelaez received her B.S. in Elementary Education from New York University. After graduating, she taught at The Spence School in NYC for ten years and then moved her growing family to New Jersey. In 2002, Antonia joined the faculty at The Peck School in Morristown. During her 20 years in education she has taught every grade from kindergarten to 4th. At Peck, she has been a member of the Faculty Team for InDeCoRe Values since its conception as well as a faculty leader for the InDeCoRe Executive Team.

The Four Respects

Greensboro Day School • Greensboro, North Carolina
Michelle Bostian, MSW, LCSW

Greensboro Day School opened its doors September 14, 1970 to 95 students. The group of parents who were at its grassroots believed this independent school would provide their children with educational excellence and at the same time be advocates for social justice in the community. Today, Greensboro Day School is a nationally respected school of over 880 students with programming from its four-year-old program through twelfth grade. The mission of Greensboro Day School is to develop the intellectual, ethical and interpersonal foundations students need to become constructive contributors to the world.

The Program and How the Process Began

The Four Respects and Second Step programs were both initiated with similar goals: foundations for behavior and development of social emotional skills to support problem solving, perspective taking, and emotion management. The primary goal at Greensboro Day School was to help students develop and use compassionate behaviors in their collaboration with others to become positive contributors to the world. It was essential that the programming be suitable for all cultures and religions. Positive character development requires a core of strong ethical values, which is needed to guide both interpersonal and intrapersonal behaviors. These core values are achieved through direct instruction and modeling of the behaviors addressed in the Four Respects and Second Step programs. These behaviors include respect for self, others, property, and time, as well as development of empathy, impulse control, and anger management skills.

The Four Respects was brought to Greensboro Day School by an administrator from Sycamore School in Indianapolis, Indiana. It resulted from the thorough work of a task force charged with the responsibility to develop a foundation for behavior and support of a positive social climate. The Four Respects was successful at Sycamore School and was easily integrated into Greensboro Day School with its simple concepts and universal language. In addition to utilizing the Four Respects, Greensboro Day School counselors researched available social emotional programs that could be integrated into existing curriculum and interwoven into the social environment of the school. Second Step, a research-based program with both prevention and practice components, was chosen. Second Step was designed to develop emotion management, perspective taking, and problem solving. It was important to have a foundation for behavior that could be easily understood both at home and school, with simple concepts and yet far reaching benefits. These two programs work synergistically to create the uniquely warm and accountable school community of Greensboro Day School.

What the Four Respects & Second Step Look Like and How They Work

The "Four Respects," an established program utilized in the Lower School of Greensboro Day School, provides students with a well-known and embedded set of core values. All behaviors can be defined and understood in relationship to:

1. Respect for Self
2. Respect for Others
3. Respect for Property
4. Respect for Time

As early as the four-year-old program, teachers help students understand and reflect on what it means to respect yourself, others, property and time. When a student needs redirection around causing a classmate's block tower to tumble, her teacher might say, "Susan, when you knocked over Henry's blocks he felt sad. When we show respect for others, we do not touch their toys without asking. Now it's time to show respect for Henry's feelings. How can you let him know you care about his feelings?" The student response will vary depending on the development of his or her empathy skills but is expected at least to include an apology and an effort to make amends.

> " *As early as the four-year-old program, teachers help students understand and reflect on what it means to respect yourself, others, property and time.* "

By the fourth or fifth grade, students have integrated the concepts and are ready to take them to a deeper level. A student of this age who walks down the hall and tears a child's artwork off the wall will be asked to think about all Four Respects.

- He did not show respect for himself by behaving in a way that is out of character or not his typical behavior.

- He did not show respect for others by touching their belongings without permission.

- He did not show respect for property by tearing the artwork off the wall and damaging it.

- He did not show respect for time, due to the time it takes to discuss the problem. This takes away from his own class time and the teacher's time in addressing the issue.

- He will be further asked to consider the other people he may not be respecting by his behavior (his parents, peers, and school leadership).

When children are compassionately able to understand the impact of their behavior on others, they are equipped to change their own behavior. The Four Respects gives students the tools to do this. It provides a common language to define behavior and its impact on others, making it easy to communicate between parents, faculty and students. Parents use the Four Respects as an effective communication tool to address concerns with their children at home. It is simple to use and easy to remember, which makes consistency a breeze.

In addition to the Four Respects, Greensboro Day School utilizes Second Step, a program created by the Committee for Children. Second Step is a research-based program teaching students the social/emotional skills of problem solving, perspective taking and emotion management.

This program is taught weekly in every classroom from the four-year-old program through the fifth grade, facilitated by the classroom teacher or teacher's assistant. Teachers can connect the Second Step program as they move through classroom lessons and daily experiences with students. Children learn problem solving, perspective taking and emotion management in a developmentally appropriate way. For example, in a kindergarten classroom a large photo may be shown to demonstrate a social situation. Children are asked to look at the photo and talk about what they see. The lesson is scripted for the teacher guiding the students through the process of understanding the possible situations that may be represented in the photo and the possible feelings of the participants. The older grades participate in lessons that challenge them to understand a greater variety of feelings as well as how children can have multiple feelings at one time. Students may be anxious about speaking in front of the class and simultaneously excited to have the moment in the spotlight. Understanding this complicated emotional experience is an objective of this program. This knowledge will facilitate healthy coping skills when students are faced with both the desire to feel the pride of accomplishment and the temptation to cheat. The skills learned are life skills, which equip children to make ethical decisions from which they grow.

> *The older grades participate in lessons that challenge them to understand a greater variety of feelings as well as how children can have multiple feelings at one time.*

Similar to the Four Respects, the Second Step program has a common language that can be used by teachers, students and parents. One phrase commonly echoed in the hallways and classrooms is the reference to the "neutral problem statement." Children are taught to see that "two children fighting over one ball" can be understood as "there is only one ball and there are two children." In helping students work through interpersonal and ethical dilemmas, this common language may also include

"I wonder what your friend might be feeling right now?" The principles learned in Second Step have shaped the culture of caring at Greensboro Day School. Thinking about the perspectives and feelings of others, as well as taking time to consider our own experiences, provides the foundations for supporting and appreciating diversity and building relationships among students and parents.

The Second Step program is integrated into curriculum through teachers extending the lessons into existing academic curriculum. For example, while having a fifth grade literature discussions about the book *When Zachary Beaver Came to Town*, by Kimberly Willis, the teacher might ask students to consider how two individuals often have different feelings about the same situation. Another example can be found in first grade, as students are asked to write in their journals about the Second Step lesson they have learned each week. In third grade, teachers build on perspective taking skills as they teach about Native Americans and the history of their experience in America. Perspective taking, and the empathy that can result from it, are nurtured through every conversation teachers facilitate about diversity in our classrooms and community.

> *Perspective taking, and the empathy that can result from it, are nurtured through every conversation teachers facilitate about diversity in our classrooms and community.*

Faculty members are regularly provided professional development on how to use the Four Respects and the Second Step programs. Through faculty meetings and ongoing conversations with the school counselor, faculty members often share examples or stories of how the Four Respects have been used to connect with students and to guide appropriate behavior. Parent education supporting use of the Four Respects is facilitated at parent nights and through conversations with school leadership and classroom teachers as well as the Lower School counselor. The school counselor also provides training for teachers in how to use the Second Step program effectively and provides ongoing support in finding ways to expound on the messages and concepts presented.

Assessing Progress

In the spring of 2012, a survey was created to assess how often students hear teachers referencing the Four Respects and how often faculty hear other students using the common language of the Four Respects. In this recent survey, 55% of students reported that they hear their teacher talk about the Four Respects every day in their classrooms. This common language, and the core value of respect, ensures the program's success at Greensboro Day School. The Four Respects are also evaluated informally through conversations with students, asking them periodically what the Four Respects are and what they mean.

Informal assessments for the effectiveness of the Second Step program are completed through conversations with students, parents and teachers. Parents frequently talk about the usefulness of the skills the children are integrating in terms of problem solving and perspective taking. Student and teacher surveys have recently been completed as well. Sixty percent of students surveyed believe the Second Step lessons have an impact on how students behave. Seventy-three percent of teachers surveyed claim to notice a benefit in the classroom because of the lessons. This data was obtained spring 2012 and will be assessed biannually.

The counseling department meets regularly to review and challenge the effectiveness of all social emotional programming at Greensboro Day School. Innovative ways to enhance current curricula are discussed and shared with faculty through educational presentations and collaborative meetings. The counselor also meets with school leadership weekly to discuss students of concern, and helps develop support plans for particular students, their families, or faculty. Support may be provided through individual, group, family or even whole class lessons designed around specific needs.

> **"** *Innovative ways to enhance current curricula are discussed and shared with faculty through educational presentations and collaborative meetings.* **"**

The mission statement at Greensboro Day School provides both an identity and a detailed path, and holds the school accountable to achieve what it states. Constructive contributors that have both intellectual and interpersonal skills need the foundations of compassion and the framework of an ethical approach to reach the goals set forward by the school.

The Four Respects and the Second Step Program are paramount in the sense of sanctuary hallmarking the community of Greensboro Day School. Second Step provides the foundational skills all children need to grow both socially and academically. These understandings enable student growth in empathy, a true twenty-first century skill. First the students learn to identify feelings in themselves, then in others. Students develop empathy for others and learn self-calming techniques along with problem solving skills. This foundation is what enables students to fully develop and internalize essential values—values that support the development of students into ethical leaders with strong interpersonal skills, who can become constructive contributors to the world.

Michelle Bostian, MSW, LCSW is the head of the counseling department and the Lower School counselor at Greensboro Day School. She has been a Licensed Clinical Social Worker since 1995. Michelle has a BS from University of North Carolina at Greensboro and a Master of Social Work from University of Illinois at Chicago. While working in her private counseling practice and volunteering in schools she discovered her passion for addressing and preventing bullying. Michelle came to Greensboro Day School as a volunteer in 2006. She soon began contract work and has been full time since 2008. Michelle is married and has three children, ages 15, 13 and 10.

C.A.R.E. Program

Breck School • Minneapolis, Minnesota
Peg Bailey, M.A. & Lisa Lokke, M.Ed.

Founded in 1886, Breck is an Episcopal, coeducational, college-preparatory day school enrolling students of diverse backgrounds and abilities in grades preschool through twelve. Breck has a long-standing tradition of offering a strong academic program, attention to spiritual development, and commitment to service. The school's mission is to:

- prepare each student for a college whose culture is compatible with the individual's needs, interests, and abilities.

- help develop each student's unique talents and potential to excel by nurturing independence and self-worth.

- instill in each student a deep sense of social responsibility.

Breck is located on a 50 acre campus in Minneapolis, Minnesota. The campus is notable for its beauty and for the fact that it houses all students in a single building, which cultivates extraordinary relationships among students and faculty, provides for collaboration among teachers across grade levels, and allows students to move easily between divisions to meet their academic needs. Breck teachers are dedicated, maintain a culture of high expectations, and provide individualized attention to students. Professional development is encouraged by a supportive board of trustees, resulting in teachers who are engaged in professional conversation with colleagues across the country as well as seekers of innovative ideas to bring to their classrooms. There are approximately 400 students in each division (Lower, Middle and Upper). The parent community actively supports the school's mission and values, and shares responsibility for the educational life of students.

The Breck curriculum is comprehensive, dynamic, and multi-faceted. Lower School students engage in all core subjects while studying modern language, visual arts, physical education, religion, media literacy, and performing arts. As students move into Middle School, they experience increased rigor in the classroom and expectations for independent work habits. In Upper School, students find a rich tapestry of courses to pursue a liberal arts education. Innovative courses are reflected in offerings in bioethics, world religions, and robotics. Multicultural education and service learning are integral throughout a student's experience. Signature programs include advanced science and history research, the one:one laptop initiative, Project Adventure, and the C.A.R.E. program.

The Program and How the Process Began

C.A.R.E. (Character Always Respect Everyday) is a character education program developed by the Lower School faculty. The program supports the mission and values of the school by instilling in students a sense of self-confidence and responsibility that comes with the development of strong character and ethical values. The goals of the C.A.R.E. program are to:

- Promote the development of strong character in students.

- Bring the community together around common character traits.

- Develop consistency with respect to the teaching of character education skills.

- Provide common language throughout the community.

- Empower students with tools to become responsible citizens.

Each month, the Lower School community invites students to participate in lessons and/or activities that promote the development of character traits, including respect, responsibility and friendship. The C.A.R.E. curriculum is integrated into morning meetings and across disciplines, and emerges in every facet of the day. In partnership with the school, parents play a key role in helping students internalize the character traits. Supporting C.A.R.E. at home is an important part of the program.

In 2002, a task force was convened to explore the needs of Lower School students in the social/emotional domain and to examine current programs and strategies to address those needs. Initial discussion focused on the creation of a developmental guidance curriculum to teach pro-social skills. For several years, Lower School teachers implemented the Responsive Classroom program as a way to support children as they transitioned to school and to build community within the classroom. Conversations were a mechanism for fostering communication and strengthening social skills. Building on this structure, further discussion led to the value of character education and providing young children with experiences to develop strong character traits. Thus, a three-pronged approach was formulated:

> *In 2002, a task force was convened to explore the needs of Lower School students in the social/emotional domain and to examine the current programs and strategies to address those needs.*

- Responsive Classroom: Classroom lessons build community within the classroom and support academic and social achievement.

- Developmental Guidance Lessons: Classroom-based lessons in the social/ emotional domain are facilitated by the Lower School counselor.

- C.A.R.E.: Character education curriculum is designed to infuse values and habits of goodness into daily conversations at school and at home.

The development of the C.A.R.E. program involved a series of stages:

Stage 1: Conduct research of existing character education programs and resource materials. Inquiries were made to public, private, and independent schools, online resources were gathered, and professional books were purchased.

Stage 2: Articulate over-arching goals of the C.A.R.E. program and student learnings.

Stage 3: Create a model for character education: classroom lessons, monthly themes, parent involvement, community participation, teacher training, resources, program assessment.

Stage 4: Identify seven character traits as "pillars" for the initial year of C.A.R.E.

Stage 5: Develop program materials: resource packets for teachers with ideas/materials for teaching character education in the classroom, a home-school component to engage parent support, monthly communication tools, meeting agendas, and strategies for faculty involvement.

Stage 6: Discuss assessment of the effectiveness of the C.A.R.E. program and plan for continued development and implementation.

When the C.A.R.E. program launched in 2004, everyone in the community made a commitment to use the character traits as touchstones for conversation. Classroom activities, dinner table talk, and community gatherings provided opportunities for students to explore the meaning of each trait and reflect on how to live with C.A.R.E. The C.A.R.E. program has far outreached the expectations the school had for instilling strong values in the children and throughout the community.

What C.A.R.E. Looks Like and How It Works

For a character education program to be truly successful, it must be embraced and internalized by the students. The launching and continuation of C.A.R.E. keeps this fact at the heart of the program. Each month, students kick off the new character trait during Lower School Community Meeting. This is a much anticipated ritual as different groups of students take the stage each month to introduce and explain the new monthly trait by singing songs, acting in skits, reading books, dancing, or even showing a video they've created. The enthusiasm is high as the motivation to implement the new trait transfers from the Lower School meeting into classrooms, where teachers continue the lessons and hold students to the expectations addressed. Although the traits are introduced to all grade levels at the same time and in the same energetic, student-driven manner, the teachers

> *For a character education program to be truly successful, it must be embraced and internalized by the students.*

then tailor the discussions and activities to the students in their specific classrooms. Listed is a sampling of the way the information is transferred into each grade level as reported by the teachers and students.

• PreK/K focus on introducing themes in developmentally appropriate ways so young children understand and internalize the meaning and importance of each theme. Strategies used include read-aloud books, bulletin boards, circle time discussions, poem sharing, songs, and art projects, all of which emphasize the C.A.R.E. themes.

• Grades One/Two experience the character themes building on previous experiences. Students add many of their own thoughts, ideas and writings to the classroom C.A.R.E. bulletin boards, journal about their understanding and ideas regarding good character, and participate in special C.A.R.E. projects.

• Grades Three/Four integrate the C.A.R.E. themes into their core curricular research projects and into their everyday lives. This is done by analyzing famous quotes to discover C.A.R.E. traits from past and present, by utilizing traits as springboards for a variety of writing projects, by incorporating C.A.R.E. themes into students' blogs, by seeking examples of historical figures who demonstrate strong character traits while doing hero/shero research projects, and by demonstrating good character while mentoring younger students.

From 2004-2012, thirty-five character traits have formed the monthly C.A.R.E. themes, with respect, responsibility and friendship repeating every year:

Respect	Responsibility	Friendship	Dependability
Honesty	Courage	Citizenship	Cooperation
Gratitude	Patience	Kindness	Perseverance
Optimism	Generosity	Attitude	Compassion
Acceptance	Stewardship	Curiosity	Appreciation
Humility	Teamwork	Flexibility	Personal Best
Creativity	Self-Control	Loyalty	Determination
Forgiveness	Understanding	Courtesy	Joyfulness
Trust	Resourcefulness	Peacefulness	

C.A.R.E. teachings don't end at school, they continue in the home. To promote home involvement, a newsletter or blog introducing the monthly character trait is posted each month for parents to read. The definition or quote used to explain the trait to students is shared to promote communication at home. The large banner outside the Lower School entrance serves as a reminder to parents and promotes the home/school connection. The library also gets involved by creating a rotating C.A.R.E. section each month so parents and students can check books out to read at home.

Since the implementation of C.A.R.E., teacher participation and ownership have been key components to its success. To sustain and enrich the program, this is paramount. To that end, a group of teachers representing each Lower School team form the C.A.R.E. Committee. This committee meets periodically throughout the year to brainstorm new ways to enhance and maintain positive momentum for the program. Responsibilities of the committee include:

> **" [The C.A.R.E. Committee] meets periodically throughout the year to brainstorm new ways to enhance and maintain positive momentum for the program. "**

- sharing information regarding C.A.R.E. with teams and bringing information back to the committee.

- selecting new character traits each year. These ideas have been compiled throughout the years by surveying the entire faculty through a brainstorming exercise at the end-of-year division meeting, handing out a paper questionnaire, or through discussions with the team representatives. After much discussion, the C.A.R.E. committee members make the final trait selections for the upcoming year.

- creating unique definitions, phrases or questions for each character trait so all students hear the same message and share the same vocabulary.

- planning and organizing students to present the C.A.R.E. themes at community meetings.

- brainstorming ideas to inspire the C.A.R.E. program.

- monitoring, evaluating and maintaining consistency in how C.A.R.E. is implemented at Breck School.

Assessing Progress

Documenting and evaluating the effectiveness of C.A.R.E. is an ongoing process. To get a true assessment the school looks to those involved: teachers, students, parents. Each year, teachers archive how they have empowered students through their implementation of the C.A.R.E program by collecting samples of student projects, taking pictures to post on a C.A.R.E. internal website, sharing classroom ideas with teams, and blogging about activities.

Students have come to anticipate discussions and activities based on the importance of good character in school. They demonstrate their understanding of key concepts through their words and actions. C.A.R.E. gives every student, preschool through fourth grade, a shared vocabulary and common expectations for themselves and those around them. Their understanding is evident in meaningful classroom discussions, effective student interactions, personal writings, and counselor visits.

To more formally evaluate student understanding of what C.A.R.E. is and why it is important, a survey was conducted. Below are three sample questions and student responses.

What is the C.A.R.E. program?

- "The C.A.R.E. program helps you remember to care more about the people around you and the community."

- "C.A.R.E. is a reminder to be responsible and how you should behave."

Do you talk about the C.A.R.E. themes at home with your family?

- "I talk to my parents about it—I even bring it up."

- "We talk about C.A.R.E. themes at dinner time."

- "We have a C.A.R.E. theme in our home that goes with the themes at school."

From your perspective, how do our C.A.R.E. themes make the community a better place for all?

- "It helps everyone think about what we are doing and take personal responsibility for our actions."

- "C.A.R.E. gives us a chance to think about how to act."

- "If we are doing something wrong and we see the right behavior, it reminds us what to do."

- "It gives us a common language as a community."

The C.A.R.E. program has sustained energy and enthusiasm since its "grass roots inception." Today, three of the initial set of character traits recur each year and form the foundation of the C.A.R.E. program: respect, responsibility, and friendship.

For the past eight years, C.A.R.E. has been a signature program in Lower School. When asked to reflect on the value of character education, teachers offered their insights:

The C.A.R.E. program . . .

- "has given us common language in the community."

- "is responsive to children's needs."

- "is universally seen in the classrooms … it is living and dynamic."

- "builds social responsibility and an awareness of others."

- "teaches important skills to develop and practice."

- "has given parents an opportunity to partner with the school and feel valued."

- "The C.A.R.E. program reflects our value of the whole child. It is a framework for building an understanding of the community's values. C.A.R.E. is a curriculum that provides a version of an 'anchor lesson'—similar to what you might do in any curricular area—that allows all teachers in the school to look for authentic ways to extend, deepen, and reinforce that concept. The fact that it is school-wide makes it that much more powerful and ce-ments our bonds as a community."

Peg Bailey, M.A., is director of the Lower School at Breck School. In her tenure as an educator, she has been a classroom teacher, resource teacher in gifted education, department chair, and administrator in both public and independent schools. She has served as a board member for the Minnesota

Children's Museum. Her primary interests include curriculum and program development. She holds a B.A. from Drake University and an M.A. from the University of Minnesota. The C.A.R.E. Program has been a rewarding and collaborative effort with faculty, parents, and students.

Lisa Lokke, M.Ed., *has enjoyed working with students, parents and faculty as guidance counselor at Breck School since 2002. She began her career in education in 1991 teaching first in Duluth, Minnesota then in Houston, Texas where she was elected "Educator of the Year" by the Parent/Teacher Association. In 1996, she transitioned to the role of counselor. Since the beginning of her career, she has focused on developing a common understanding of positive character traits in students. Ms. Lokke is the proud mother of three children and spends her free time camping, hiking and running.*